# BRAVO!

## Poems About Amazing Hispanics

**Margarita Engle**

✦

illustrated by
**Rafael López**

**GODWIN BOOKS**

Henry Holt and Company ✦ New York

*In memory of Dr. Tomás Rivera,*
*my creative writing professor*
*—M. E.*

*To heroes in the making,*
*who come in different colors, shapes, and sizes*
*—R. L.*

## ACKNOWLEDGMENTS

I thank God for amazing people from all backgrounds. Joyful thanks to my family; my editor, Laura Godwin, who lit the spark; Julia Sooy; my agent, Michelle Humphrey, who helped tend the flames; the marvelous writer Alma Flor Ada for proofreading; Debbie Reese for proofreading the poem about Fabiola Cabeza de Baca, who worked with Pueblo nations in New Mexico; and Rafael López for beautiful artwork.

Henry Holt and Company
*Publishers since 1866*
175 Fifth Avenue
New York, New York 10010
mackids.com

Henry Holt® is a registered trademark of Macmillan Publishing Group, LLC.
Text copyright © 2017 by Margarita Engle
Illustrations copyright © 2017 by Rafael López
All rights reserved.

Library of Congress Cataloging-in-Publication Data
Names: Engle, Margarita, author. | López, Rafael, 1961– illustrator.
Title: Bravo! / Margarita Engle, Rafael López.
Description: New York : Henry Holt and Company, [2016]
Identifiers: LCCN 2016009015 | ISBN 9780805098761 (hardcover)
Subjects: LCSH: Latin Americans—Biography—Juvenile literature. | Hispanic Americans—
Biography—Juvenile literature.
Classification: LCC E184.S75 E715 2016 | DDC 920.0092/68073—dc23
LC record available at https://lccn.loc.gov/2016009015

Our books may be purchased in bulk for promotional, educational, or business use.
Please contact your local bookseller or the Macmillan Corporate and Premium Sales Department at
(800) 221-7945 ext. 5442 or by e-mail at MacmillanSpecialMarkets@macmillan.com.

First Edition—2017
The illustrations for this book were created using a combination of acrylic on wood, pen and ink,
watercolor, construction paper, and Adobe Photoshop.
Printed in China by Toppan Leefung Printing Ltd., Dongguan City, Guangdong Province

1  3  5  7  9  10  8  6  4  2

Dear Readers,

This is not a book about the most famous Hispanics. These poems are about a variety of amazing people who lived in geographic regions now included in the modern United States. They are people who have faced life's challenges in creative ways. Some were celebrated in their lifetimes but have been forgotten by history. Others achieved lasting fame.

Many Hispanic Americans are immigrants, refugees, or exiles. Others were born in the United States but retain strong ties with the languages and cultures of ancestral lands. Some Hispanics are descendants of people who stayed in one place while their homelands changed from Spanish colonies to Mexican territories, and, eventually, to states within the US. Puerto Ricans are in the unique position of being citizens of the United States, without statehood. Some Hispanics speak only English or only Spanish, but many are bilingual or trilingual, with knowledge of indigenous languages such as Mixteca, Maya, and Quechua.

For simplicity, I have listed modern names for regions of family ancestry before each poem rather than using historic names such as New Spain. If you want to know a bit more about these amazing people, please read Notes About the Lives at the end of this book.

Your friend/ *tu amiga*,
Margarita Engle

# JUAN DE MIRALLES

1713–1780
Cuba

## FIRST FRIEND

I believe in the good cause
of American independence from England.
Thousands of soldiers from Spain
and all the regions of Latin America
are fighting side by side
with George Washington's men,
as we struggle to defeat the British.

George Washington is my close friend.
We've ridden together in parades, and last year
we celebrated a festive New Year's Eve
at my home in Philadelphia.

Now, in deep snow, soldiers at Yorktown
are starving, their teeth weakened by scurvy,
a disease that can only be cured
with fresh fruit.

George asks me to help by sending my ships
back to the island of Cuba—my homeland—
so that I can deliver a fragrant load of juicy green
tropical limes
and tasty
pink guavas.

Fresh fruit really is the cure for scurvy.
Soon, the soldiers are saved from illness,
and when they fight, they win
our battle against the British.

Sometimes friendship
is the sweetest form
of courage.

# FÉLIX VARELA

1788–1853
Cuba

# CHOOSING PEACE

My family's tradition is fighting.
I am expected to become a soldier.
By the age of fourteen, I know that I will never
fire a gun, or carry a sword.

I do not wish to kill men, so instead, I read,
study, teach, and when I decide to be a priest,
I preach against cruelty, speaking out in favor
of freedom for slaves, and freedom
for the colonies of Spain.

Demanding justice is dangerous!
Forced to flee my homeland, I'm followed
by an assassin, but when I speak to him
of kindness, he listens,
choosing peace.

As an exile in New York, I become the priest
at a church attended by survivors
of the horrible famine that sends
thousands of Irish families
fleeing starvation,
seeking refuge
in the United States.

I work hard to help Irish families build schools
for their children, and I tend cholera patients,
and I defend Irish American boys and girls
against insults from mobs
who hate them
just because their parents
are immigrants.

# JUANA BRIONES

1802–1889
Mexico

## ON MY OWN

I was born in Alta California
when it still belonged to Spain.

This is a land of good herbs
and great sorrows—the conquest
of *los indios*, my soldier-husband's
cruel job.

When he hits me, I leave him,
and for many years, first under Spanish rule,
then Mexican, and now American,
I survive as a rancher and healer,
curing the sick with medicinal plants,
and healing myself
with independence.

# PAULINA PEDROSO

1845–1925
Cuba

# EQUAL RIGHTS

José Martí and all the other exiled poets
meet in my Florida home, where they recite
beautiful verses, and discuss ways to bring freedom
to our homeland.

They call me a heroine for creating
a friendship society of black and white *cubanos*,
all of us living in exile, where we help each other,
and help the needy—orphans, widows, the poor . . .

When my friend and I walk arm in arm,
it is a wordless statement of equality,
Martí's light skin and my dark skin
side by side.

## JOSÉ MARTÍ

1853–1895
Cuba

# THE MAGIC OF WORDS

As a child on the island, I see injustice,
so I write about freedom, but at sixteen,
I'm arrested, and after months of hard labor
in prison, I am forced to flee my homeland.

In New York, I stroll through Central Park
with the children of other exiles, telling stories
of gentle elephants and enchanted shrimp . . .

I say that each day is a poem.
Some hours are green and peaceful.
Others are red, like festivals or storms.
I love teaching children how to tell
their own stories.

# WILD EXPLORATION

Childhood is so difficult when your parents
fight. He is from Mexico, she is American,
I am both. They separate, we move,
I try and try to hope that they'll
reunite.

But when I'm all grown up and really quite old,
I finally figure out how to feel useful,
enjoying the adventure of a two-country life.

I go to college in California, study botany,
and then set out to explore jungles
all over Mexico and South America,
collecting fascinating plants
that are completely new
to science!

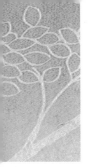

# LOUIS AGASSIZ FUERTES

**1874–1927**
**Puerto Rico**

## LET THE BIRDS LIVE!

Ever since I was little, I knew
that I wanted to paint pictures of birds.

I love the beauty and freedom of wings.
Other artists kill birds to make them easy
to pose, but I want to let the birds live!

So I learn to paint quickly, while wild creatures
fly swiftly, high overhead in the wide
wondrous
sky.

## AÍDA DE ACOSTA

1884–1962
Cuba

# THE WoRLD'S FiRST WOMAN PiLOT

Airships!
The thrill of seeing a man in a basket,
dangling beneath a huge balloon, as he circles
the Eiffel Tower here in Paris, so far
from my New Jersey home.

Lessons!
I love the excitement of learning to soar.

Flight!
I'm the first woman pilot, but I won't be the last—
every little girl who sees me up here in blue sky
will surely grow up with dreams
of flying too!

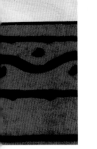

# FABIOLA CABEZA DE BACA

1894–1991
Mexico

# A RECIPE FOR STRENGTH

My *familia* came to this land
over four hundred years ago.
Some were brutal conquerors, but now
most people are *mestizo*, mixed-race,
part *indio*, neighbors
and friends.

When I teach children all over New Mexico,
I speak to them in English, Spanish, Tewa, and Tiwa.
In my cookbooks, I keep the old recipes, making sure
that new ways of cooking homegrown food
are healthy.

Whatever is left over can be canned and sold.
When women earn our own money,
we feel strong
and independent.

## ARNOLD ROJAS

1898–1988
Mexico

# LiFE ON HORSEBACK

My Mexican ancestors
included Yaqui and Maya *indios*,
people who fought to stay free
and live in their own
traditional ways.

But I did not feel free when I was a farmworker.
I hated picking oranges in the orchards
of Southern California, so I moved north
to the Central Valley, where I learned
the horsemanship skills
of *un vaquero*—a cowboy.
Roping. Riding. Roundups.
To learn, I had to listen to older men,
and now I'm the one telling stories
about my life of adventure
on horseback.

## PURA BELPRÉ

1899–1982
Puerto Rico

# TWO LANGUAGES
# AT THE LIBRARY

My journey to Nueva York
has been a voyage made of stories
that grow.

I came to attend my sister's wedding,
but I stayed, found work, and studied
to become a children's librarian—the first
*puertorriqueña* ever hired in the entire
New York Public Library system!

How strange that I am the first, in this city
with so many two-language children who are
so eager to read, so happy to learn . . .

Nothing makes me feel more satisfied
than a smile on the face of a child who holds
an open book.

# HELPING WILD ANIMALS

As the first chief of the Wildlife Division for America's national parks, I travel all over the United States, studying rare animals.

I convince Congress to stop letting national park rangers kill mountain lions and other predators.

Let us save rare species before it is too late!

# JULIA DE BURGOS

1914–1953
Puerto Rico

# MY RIVER OF DREAMS

Six of my twelve brothers and sisters
died of hunger, but my gentle mother
took me for long walks
beside a river
of beautiful dreams.

I learned to love nature and the island,
even though we were so poor that I
had to climb into classrooms
through a window, because we
could not afford school tuition.

I struggled to become a teacher
and a poet, so I could use words
to fight for equal rights for women,
and work toward meeting
the needs of poor children,

and speak of independence
for Puerto Rico.

Later, much later,
even though I now live
in New York,
I still remember
my own childhood's
beautiful river
of dreams.

# SOLVING MEDICAL MYSTERIES

My struggle to breathe
makes me long to be a doctor,
learning how to heal
asthma.

Allergies.
Diseases.
Rare disorders
and common ones.

Research in a laboratory
is the key to creating
new medicines,
new cures.

# TITO PUENTE

1923–2000
Puerto Rico

# BRAVE MUSIC

When I was a small child
at home in New York,
neighbors complained
because I drummed
on pots,
pans,
windows,
and walls.

They said I was too noisy,
too lively,
too energetic,
too wild . . .

Now they call me the King of Latin Jazz,
and no one thinks my bold music
is noise!

# SHARING PEACE

After we lost our own farm,
we had to work in other fields,
moving from crop to crop, harvesting
fruits and vegetables.

No bathrooms. No water. No shady
moments of rest. I longed to be treated
with dignity and respect.

Now, as an adult, I still see the need
for change, but I don't believe
in fighting with weapons or fists,
so change comes slowly, as I lead
other farmworkers
in nonviolent protests,
marches, strikes, boycotts,
and voting.

# SHARING HOPE

When I was a child on the island, I worked
delivering milk cans, while my father
was working in the sugar fields.

Whenever I had a free moment,
I played *béisbol*, a game that gave me
happiness and hope. Now I play
for the Pittsburgh Pirates.

Most people up here in the North
are friendly, but some treat me
different, because of my dark skin.

I believe in equality, and I believe
in sharing hope,
so whenever I hear

of a disaster, like an earthquake,
I organize a delivery
of medicine and food.

Fame has given me a chance
to show how baseball is not
the only part of life that needs
teamwork.

# TOMÁS RIVERA

1935–1984
Mexico

# COURAGEOUS POETRY

My family follows the crops.
We move from field to field.

Bend. Plant. Harvest.
How will I ever finish
school?

Reading comforts me.
I find magazines in trash piles.
Reading leads to writing.
I find poetry in tomato fields,
and stories in the faces
of weary workers.

I read, and I write, and I study
until I am the first Latino leader
of a University of California campus.

Students often tell me they feel
inspired by my own
life story.

Sometimes the best way to teach
is by example.

# MORE AND MORE AMAZING LATINOS

So many, so varied, such a beautiful
mixture of dreams!

Sonia Sotomayor from New York's Puerto Rican
community, first Latino ever appointed
to the Supreme Court.

Rosemary Casals, Salvadoran American tennis star
who demanded equal pay for women,
and Julia Marino,
Paraguayan American Olympic skier,
Juan Rodríguez, Puerto Rican golf champion
who grew up so poor that his first golf club
was a guava branch, his first ball
a crushed tin can.

César Pelli, Argentine American architect,
Bruno Fonseca, Uruguayan American artist,

and so many actors: América Ferrara,
Honduran American; and Benjamin Bratt,
Peruvian American; and Zoe Saldana,

Dominican American; and the singer
Christina Aguilera, Ecuadorian Irish American;
along with other musicians too—but not just rock stars—
Martina Arroyo, Puerto Rican opera singer;
Gustavo Dudamel, Venezuelan American
symphony orchestra conductor;
José Feliciano, the Puerto Rican folksinger
who fought for the right of blind people
to take their guide dogs on airplanes;
and Sixto Rodríguez, a Mexican American
songwriter whose poetic words inspired
freedom for all
in distant South Africa,
and Tony Meléndez, the award-winning
Nicaraguan American guitarist who plays
with his feet, because he was born without arms.

You can see Soledad O'Brien on television,
the African Cuban Australian American newscaster
who refused to change her mixed-together name . . .

and no matter which field of science interests you,
there will be someone to admire:
Franklin Chang Díaz, Chinese Costa Rican American
astronaut, the first Latino in space,

and Ellen Ochoa, Mexican American astronaut,
the first Latina to soar gravity-free . . .

Mireya Mayor, Cuban American gorilla scientist,
the first woman National Geographic Explorer,

Adriana Ocampo,
Colombian American planetary geologist
for NASA, an expert on the rocks
of outer space,

Olga Linares, Panamanian American
archaeologist, and John Joaquín Muñoz,
Guatemalan American medical researcher,
and Matías Duarte, Chilean American
computer software inventor at Google,

Jaime Escalante, Bolivian American
mathematician, dedicated to teaching,
and Juan Felipe Herrera, the first Latino
United States Poet Laureate!

Imagine a time when a Latino writer
reads his own heartfelt words
at the inauguration
of an American president—
it already happened!
Richard Blanco, openly gay
Cuban American poet, bravely stood
in front of Barack Obama,
and millions of people,
to read verses that praise
the great nation
that welcomed
his refugee
parents.
*¡Bravo!*

# NOTES ABOUT THE LIVES

## Juan de Miralles
### 1713–1780

Born in Spain, Juan de Miralles moved to Cuba as a young boy, married into a Cuban family, and

became such a successful merchant that the king of Spain sent him to help American revolutionaries and to serve as an observer. During a secret meeting with Patrick Henry, Miralles helped plan the strategy that defeated British troops in Florida. At the Continental Congress in Philadelphia, Miralles became friends with George Washington. He rode in military parades with Washington and Hamilton and is credited with saving troops from scurvy by delivering Cuban fruit. When Miralles died of pneumonia at Valley Forge, Washington led the military funeral procession and presided over the service. The name of Juan de Miralles is included on a plaque at St. Mary's Church in Philadelphia, along with the other Founding Fathers.

## Félix Varela
### 1788–1853

Félix Varela was born in Cuba. Orphaned at the age of six, he was sent to Florida to live with his grandfather, who expected him to be a soldier, but at the age of fourteen, he defied his family's military tradition. "I do not wish to kill men," he wrote. Varela returned to Cuba, where he became a priest, teacher, and lawmaker. After speaking out against colonial policies, he was forced to flee. As a parish priest in New York, Varela became an outspoken advocate of equal rights for Irish immigrants.

## Juana Briones
### 1802–1889

Juana Briones was born in the present-day American state of California at a time when it still belonged to Spain. During her lifetime, the region first became part of Mexico, then part of the United States. Her parents were pioneers who came to Alta California from New Spain (now Mexico) in 1776, with the De Anza Expedition. Their mixed-race heritage, with ancestors who were Spanish, African, and Native American, made it difficult to stay in mainland Mexico, an area with a strict

racial caste system. As a child and young woman, Briones learned about medicinal plants from *mestiza* (mixed-race) and Native American women in Santa Cruz and San Francisco. She became a *curandera* (healer) at a time when San Francisco was still called Yerba Buena (Good Herb). Briones married a soldier and had many children, but she separated from her husband; he was abusive. On her own, she raised cattle, sold milk and vegetables, healed people during a smallpox epidemic, and trained her nephew, who became a doctor. She adopted a Native American daughter and spoke out against widespread brutality against Native Americans. After California became a state, Juana fought in court for twelve years, struggling to keep her ranchland. Even though she did not know how to read and write, her court battle succeeded. Today, Juana Briones is known as the Founding Mother of San Francisco.

## Paulina Pedroso
### 1845–1925

As the freeborn daughter of former slaves, Paulina Pedroso was bolder than most young girls in Cuba

at that time. She married young and moved with her husband to Florida, where she worked in a cigar factory. Their home became a refuge for José Martí and other Cuban exiles who were planning the island's rebellion against colonial Spain. Together, Pedroso and Martí also spoke out against inequality in the United States, strolling arm in arm on the streets of Ybor City in Tampa, in open defiance of racial segregation.

## José Martí
### 1853–1895

José Martí was the Cuban-born son of Spanish parents. He was arrested at the age of sixteen for writing letters in favor of Cuba's independence from Spain. After six months of hard labor in a prison quarry, he was exiled, first to Spain and later to the United States. In New York, he became a celebrated poet, journalist, educator, and author of children's stories. His translations of Ralph Waldo Emerson and Walt Whitman introduced Spanish-speaking people to the American literature that influenced Latino poets. Martí died in battle, fighting for Cuba's independence from Spain.

## Ynés Mexía
### 1870–1938

As the daughter of a Mexican diplomat and an American mother, Ynés Mexía was born in Washington, DC. Her parents' stormy marriage made her childhood difficult, and Mexía lived in many places before settling in San Francisco, where she began hiking and studying botany. At the age of fifty-five, Mexía became a plant explorer, collecting plants in Mexico and South America, where she discovered five hundred new species.

## Louis Agassiz Fuertes
### 1874–1927

Born in Ithaca, New York, to a Puerto Rican father and an American mother, Louis Agassiz Fuertes was fascinated by birds. His father was an engineering professor who expected Fuertes to study

engineering, but instead he chose to become a bird artist. Fuertes went on most of the great expeditions of his time, illustrated many bird books, and painted backgrounds for the habitat groups at the American Museum of Natural History.

He pioneered the painting of living birds in natural habitats, learning to stop killing and posing them as John James Audubon did. Most ornithologists think of him as the greatest bird artist who ever lived. He is known as the Father of Modern Bird Art.

## Aída de Acosta
### 1884–1962

Aída de Acosta was the New Jersey–born daughter of a Cuban shipping executive and a Spanish

mother. At the age of nineteen, during a trip to France, she became fascinated by the newly invented dirigibles, which were called "airships." Acosta took flying lessons, then piloted an airship from Paris to a polo field over half a mile away, nearly six months before the Wright brothers flew a fixed-wing aircraft. She is known as the First Woman of Powered Flight.

## Fabiola Cabeza de Baca
### 1894–1991

Born in New Mexico, Fabiola Cabeza de Baca was a descendant of Spanish explorers who reached the region in the 1530s. As a child, she loved riding

her pony and helping with ranch chores. After high school, she convinced her father to let her become a teacher. In the classroom, she used a bilingual approach, including Latino and Native American history along with the standard curriculum.

After college, she became an Agricultural Extension Service agent and traveled all over New Mexico, teaching scientific food preservation in English and Spanish, as well as in the native Tewa and Tiwa languages. Even after losing a leg in a train accident, she continued teaching in remote villages and writing cookbooks that combined healthy food preparation with traditional recipes. Cabeza de Baca helped rural women achieve financial independence by preserving homegrown foods and selling them along with traditional handicrafts. After retiring, she trained Peace Corps volunteers and served as a United Nations representative in Mexico.

## Arnold Rojas
### 1898–1988

Arnold Rojas was born in Southern California, where he hated working as a farm laborer. To escape from picking oranges, he fled to the Central Valley, where he became a noted *vaquero* (cowboy), horse trainer, and storyteller. In his book *These Were the Vaqueros*, Rojas told how he learned about horses and cattle from older men who knew traditional Mexican *rodeo* (roundup) and *charro* (horsemanship) skills. He encouraged the preservation of Latino culture in the United States.

## Pura Belpré
### 1899–1982

Pura Belpré was born in Puerto Rico, where her studies were interrupted when she attended her sister's wedding in New York. After working in

the garment industry in that city, she became a librarian, introduced bilingual story hours, bought Spanish books, wrote her own stories, collected folktales, hosted great artists such as Diego Rivera, and became the New York Public Library system's Spanish Children's Specialist. Her memory is honored each year at the American Library Association's Pura Belpré Award Celebración for Latino children's book authors and illustrators.

## George Meléndez Wright
### 1904–1936

George Meléndez Wright's father was an American sea captain, and his mother was from El Salvador. He was born in San Francisco, where his aunt raised him after his parents died. He loved nature walks and hiking, so he studied forestry and zoology. Working as a naturalist at Yosemite National Park, he was shocked by the way animals were mistreated or even killed. Meléndez Wright proposed a wildlife survey to help prevent the extinction of rare species. When the park service could not pay for the survey, he spent his own money. As the first chief of the Wildlife Division, Meléndez Wright introduced scientific management practices that saved trumpeter swans and other endangered species from extinction. He was one of America's greatest conservationists.

## Julia de Burgos
### 1914–1953

As the oldest of thirteen children, Julia de Burgos had a difficult childhood in Puerto Rico. Six of her

siblings died of malnutrition, but she managed to stay in school and become a teacher, writer, civil rights activist, and advocate of Puerto Rican independence from the United States. After moving to New York, she suffered from depression, which led her to alcoholism. She was buried in a pauper's grave, but her remains were later moved to Puerto Rico, where she is remembered as a heroic leader and one of the island's greatest poets.

## Baruj Benacerraf
### 1920–2011

Born in Venezuela of Spanish-Moroccan-Jewish ancestry, Benacerraf spent much of his childhood  in France. His family returned to Venezuela at the onset of World War II but soon moved to New York so that he could study science and medicine. Having suffered from asthma as a child, Benacerraf focused his medical research on trying to understand the genetic basis for allergies and other immunological diseases. He became the Chair of Pathology at Harvard Medical School and received the 1980 Nobel Prize in Medicine.

## Tito Puente
### 1923–2000

 Tito Puente was born in New York's Spanish Harlem to Puerto Rican parents. Already talented as a small child, he was a professional musician by the age of thirteen, playing many instruments with such rhythm and flair that he became known as the King of Latin Jazz.

## César Chávez
### 1927–1993

As one of six children in his Mexican American family in Arizona, César Chávez started life on a farm. When his grandfather's land was lost during  the Great Depression, the family had to survive by following crops from one harvest to another, becoming migrant workers in the orchards and vineyards of California. Because Chávez loved to read, he had a chance to learn about the nonviolent protest methods of Gandhi in India. Adapting those methods to boycotts and marches, Chávez became a labor union organizer, leading farmworkers in a peaceful struggle for fair wages and safe conditions. In many parts of the United States, his memory is celebrated on March 31, César Chávez Day.

## Roberto Clemente
### 1934–1972

Born in Puerto Rico, Roberto Clemente moved to the mainland United States to play baseball. With  the Pittsburgh Pirates, he played in the 1960 and 1971 World Series. Clemente became the first Latino to reach 3,000 hits, including 240 home runs, and he received the Golden Glove Award twelve years in a row. He died in a plane crash while trying to deliver supplies to earthquake survivors in Nicaragua. A year later, he was elected to the National Baseball Hall of Fame.

## Tomás Rivera
### 1935–1984

 Tomás Rivera was born in Texas, where he followed the crops with his Mexican American farmworker family. He loved to read, and when he was twelve, he began writing. Rivera was the first member of his family to graduate from college.

He became a teacher, then went on to earn a doctorate and become a highly respected educator, poet, novelist, and the first Latino chancellor of a University of California campus.